Charlie Finds A Home!

Written By:
Martha De La Torre

Illustrations By:
Sierra Fraser

Dedicated to foster children everywhere.

And to my oldest grandson, Brandon, whose journey inspired this story and is an incredible blessing to our family.

When Charlie
was born,
he was happy
and felt loved.

But his mamma did not have enough milk to feed him and he was hungry.

She had to send him to live with another family.

When Charlie arrived,
he thought, "They do not
look like me, but they
seem very nice."

Charlie got along great with this new family. They fed him with bottles full of milk until he was all better and healthy again.

He loved dancing and singing with what his family called 'children.'

He asked,
"Am I a child?"

"No, you are not a child. But, they do call goats 'kids'."

Every day Charlie got
bigger and bigger...

Soon he got too big to live
in the house and it was
time to go live outside
with a new family.

Charlie was so excited!
"Yay! They look like me! I love
this new family of mine."

But soon Charlie realized that
his family was not like him at all.
They looked like him, but they
did not like him. They told him,
"You are not part of our family."

They would not sleep
with him. They would not
eat with him. They would not
play with him.

Charlie was so sad.

One night there was a
big Texas storm brewing,
and Charlie was scared.

He looked over to his new
family and they said,
"You can't come over here!"

The sky flashed bright and the rain started to pour!

Just then there was a loud cracking roar!

Charlie was so scared that he ran with all his might!

He ran right into a fence post.

Charlie felt dazed and stumbled away...

He was hurt, scared, and all alone.

Just then Charlie heard
someone call out to him.

"Are you okay kid?"

Charlie asked,
"Who are you?"

"I am a horse, my name is Cash.
I live here on this ranch with my
family. Who are you?"

"My name is Charlie. I am a goat!"

"Nice to meet you Charlie.
Why are you all alone?"
asked Cash.

Charlie answered,
"I don't know
where I belong."

"Why do you
think that?"
asked Cash.

Charlie answered, "I have lived with other families but it did not work out. Maybe because I didn't look like them. I did not look like the human family, and I was a different color than the goat family. They were black and white and I am brown."

The rain had stopped
and the thunder quieted...

"Well, I better be on my way,"
Charlie said.

"Where are you going?"
asked Cash.

"I'm looking for a
family that looks like
me to call my own,"
said Charlie.

"Well, we don't look like each other, but maybe we can be family," said Cash.

Charlie asked Cash,
"Why would you want to
be family with me?
No one else has."

Then Cash said, "Families are like puzzles. They can be made of different pieces, different colors and shapes. What makes them family is LOVE."

Cash walked close to Charlie and stood right next to him and said, "Family is not always what you are born into or who you look like. Family are those that love and support you, they accept you for who you are and want the best for you."

From that day on
Charlie and Cash were
family and nothing
could separate them.

The End.

About The Author

Martha De La Torre is an entrepreneur and business owner. She is the proud mother of 3 grown children and the loving grandmother of 6.

Close to retirement, she has decided to embark on her lifelong dream of being a children's author.

Acknowledgements

First and foremost I would like to thank my grandson Brandon for being the inspiration for my book and the brightest light in my life.

Thank you Sierra, my talented grand-niece who perfectly illustrated my vision and brought the pages in this book to life. I can't wait to see what you accomplish in the years to come!

Thank you to my daughter Christina, my son Joseph and my daughter-in-law Samantha for the constant encouragement. Your honest feedback and sound advice helped this book take shape much faster than if I had done it alone.

And last, but not least, I would like to thank my son Matthew and his wife Sarah for allowing me to share the stories of their family. I am grateful for the use of pictures and opening up their home and allowing me the opportunity to observe incredible relationship between Cash and Charlie, and write my story.

Made in the USA
Las Vegas, NV
19 April 2021

21729546R00019